ONE SWEET POMEGRANATE

A COLLECTION OF POEMS

By Adelina Fabiano

 FriesenPress

Suite 300 - 990 Fort St
Victoria, BC, V8V 3K2
Canada

www.friesenpress.com

ISBN
978-1-5255-7152-7 (Hardcover)
978-1-5255-7153-4 (Paperback)
978-1-5255-7154-1 (eBook)

Poetry, Subjects & Themes, Women Authors

Distributed to the trade by The Ingram Book Company

A pomegranate, a symbol of abundance and fertility in many cultures and religions, is said to give beauty to those who eat it. For me, the beauty and complexity of this fruit represents life itself. This book is a reflection, an homage, and a testament to the gift of life, this one sweet life we get to live. It is an acknowledgement of our ability to experience the here and now, however complex, fleeting, painful, or joyful. Whatever you feel in this life, may you always have permission to own it. To feel is to be alive.

These poems are my lived experience, my interpretation, my soul's expression, encompassing my past, my present, my unfolding self. Most of all, they are meant to be shared with each and every one of you. Ready to bloom.

Dedication:

This book is dedicated to my sweet grandmother, my Nonna Adelina, a true orator and poet in her own right. Thank you for always having the patience to peel us a pomegranate.

Photo of my Nonna & I, three weeks before she passed away

Table of Contents

A MORNING ESPRESSO

Long shot or short.

Rich but not too rich.

Bitter but not too bitter.

Chestnut, Chocolate, Cocoa brown.

With a biscotto makes it sweeter.

A double or a single.

Sometimes sour.

Strong on its own.

A trusted wake-up call!

Meant to be shared.

Amaro.

Amore.

Amante.

Caffè "Shakerato!"

An aroma like no other.

Straight from the earth.

No need for sugar, exquisite as it is.

Nutty.

Fruity.

Spicy.

Full.

Creamy.

Smooth or thick.

Its flavour an acquired taste.

When complete, leaves a residue at the bottom of your cup.

Whichever way you choose,

savour

every

sip.

GRATITUDE

Each morning I awake to a beautiful sunrise.

I walk outside and see nothing that is a surprise.

I breathe and take it all in.
Thanking God I am alive, I touch my skin.

So much beauty before my eyes,
this reality far from lies.

In spite of sometimes feeling sad,
I think of all the memories I've had.

Good or bad, no experience has been wasted.
What joy, tears, and love I have tasted!

TRUTH

A humble truth lies before us.
We pretend we can walk alone . . .
yet we fear the unknown.

As much as we can face the challenges ahead,
faltering now and then,
we go through life as if we were dead.

Grateful and awake,

the time is now.
Life is here for you to give or take.

RAIN

Without notice, her mood becomes grey.

Holding it in, something rubbed her the wrong way.

She slowly ruminates,

her strength and fiery spirit soon dominates.

Lightning strikes where once was mistakenly dim.

From afar they finally heard her hymn.

Brilliantly golden.

Ever so emboldened.

Her tears begin to flow,

what courage she has shown,

welcoming upon the earth a new glow.

SOLITUDE

I sit solemnly in silent solitude
wondering when the waves will calm.
I look within for a reservoir of fortitude.

Sifting through my memories gone by,
I let the tears flow freely.

There will be a better future.

I close my eyes and sigh . . .

ANOTHER DAY

Just another day, the pain has visited again.

I challenge it.

I ignore it.

I make a useless bargain.

It is here to stay.
The price I pay.

Born like this, more than skin deep.
The pain will go away, but only when I sleep.
Until I wake to another day.
Sometimes breathless, but still breathing.
Like a wandering cat led astray.
I find myself back home, feel the pulse of each heartbeat,
no longer seething.

THE TREE

Stoic Cyprus tree.

Over 2000 years old.

The faint breeze falls upon you from the sea.

Stood the test of time.

Pillaged from one land to another.

How much you have seen and heard in your lifetime?

Standing tall now to the heavens above.

Elegant and fragrant.

Meticulously manicured.

Far from vagrant.

But how easily we forget where we are from.

A new life, the past behind you.

How far you have come.

However, no matter your pursuits,

honour your humble roots.

RECOVERY

I search deep within, far beyond what I understand.

The pain I can no longer withstand.

I look back, wondering what is best for me,

only to realize it is my past from which I want to flee.

It feels like a death. I fear the future.

I must face forward in spite of this drunken stupor.

There comes a time when one must set the pain free.

Only then can you move ahead to all that you can be.

COURAGEOUSLY YOU

Hard to admit, what was there no longer exists.

Forcefully you face the truth, in spite of what your heart resists.

Courageously you go through the pain, wrenching as it can be.

Face it head on, without the urge to flee.

Courageously you accept that your path may be diverted.

One step.

One choice.

Leaving you forever converted.

IF ONLY . . .

If only I knew then what I know now . . .
I would stand strong and tall.
I wouldn't choose to hide behind that guarding wall.
I'd speak my mind, open my heart for love to allow . . .

Every breath I'd take would be deep and long.
I would trust more freely, without taking stock of those
who have done me wrong.

If only I knew then what I know now . . .

I would take more risks, make more mistakes.
Knowing in myself, no matter what,
I have the strength to mend those heartaches.

LOST

Lost.

Lonely.

Left.

Longing to be loved.

Leaving my old life behind.

Feeling scared and blind.

Many nights alone in bed,

I tuck myself to sleep.

When will it no longer pierce so deep?

Lifeless.

Lost.

Lonely.

Wondering when this pain will stop.

Every tear I shed

another moment lost

to the life I lead and the one I led.

THE ANT

An ant.

It rarely gets noticed.

Asks for little.

Takes no space.

Each one helps the other out.

We take up more space.

We take what does not belong to us.

We ask for so much. It is never enough.

We're

still

not

happy.

Why?

Have you ever stopped to ask an ant what makes it happy?

AGELESS

Do not let your age cage you in.

Like the rebirth of a new star.

Like a wound that heals itself.

Like a racing wildfire,

like a budding stem,

like a river that flows into its ocean.

Whatever social constructs.

Whatever limitations.

Today, tomorrow, begin again.

Another year passed.

More wisdom amassed.

WHY DO YOU STAY?

Do you think he loves you?

Why do you stay?

How many have you let hurt you?

Why do you stay?

Why do you go back?

You choose to hurt you, too?

Why do you stay?

TEMPORARY LOVE

When we are desperate, we seek temporary love.
Drugs, drinking, dangerous liaisons, all of the above.

Like a multiple-choice test.
Choosing every answer but the best.

Hoping to fill the sunken void.
Hoping loneliness is what we will avoid.

Only feeling worse than before.
We find ourselves up against ourselves in a war.

To seek real love, one must surrender.
Faith, trust, openness, "amore" in all its splendour.

FEAR

Truth be told.

I am afraid.

I am afraid I will find no one who will love me the way
he did.

I keep to myself.

Easier that way.

Like a self- fulfilling prophecy, my heart will forbid.

I toss and turn.

I fear what tomorrow might bring.

I welcome few.

Who will stay and listen to me sing?

Another year has passed.

If time heals all wounds, I feel myself relapsed.

I am struggling.

Hopeless and lonely.

In the same place.

I look in the mirror.

Sad eyes.

A smile no longer found on this face.

Why do I see and feel more than I can hold?

Have I become what I did not want . . . oh, so cold?

I walk forward.

Left with whatever grace.

Simply wishing love is what I can one day again embrace.

MY FRACTURED SELF

Some moments I am so sure.

Like a personified, glorified superhero.

Other times, I am just a blur.

Frozen, fractured, crippled in choice.

Somewhere, somehow, I lost my voice.

I thought I had a plan.

I seem to have it all together, don't we all?

The first to admit when things got hard, I ran.

When we choose to see life as an illusion,

All we do is retreat to complete seclusion.

SET IT FREE

Let it go, it's not for you to bear anymore.

The pain is not for you to store.

You sit alone each passing night, dreaming of your spirit in flight.

Away from all this conformity,

deep within lies some deformity.

Let yourself detach from this complexity.

Surrendering to the simplicity.

Let it go, it's time to set it free . . .

so it can go and feel its glee.

DESIGNER HANDBAGS

Modern car, designer kitchen, designer handbags, exquisite shoes.

Painted walls of various hues.

Politicians with their varying views.

Restaurants galore, abiding conventional laws.

How perfectly we can all hide our flaws.

A life meant to enjoy, yet lonesome we do feel.

What really matters? Are we keeping it real?

As you drive in your SUVs, with your designer handbags,

have you stopped to look at the homeless teen, his weathered face?

His sad eyes.

He too was once an infant, still a child, now begging with desperate pleas.

For a moment you freeze, should I or shouldn't I?

You rush home.

Granite countertops.

Netflix, HBO, Instagram. Filters of your choice. Even Skip the Dishes.

Your wish is your command. Your command becomes your wishes.

For some, a double garage is still not enough.

A double-edged sword.

Who is really the one handcuffed?

Consumption is our MO.

The truth is, you're just a Joe Blow.

No different than that homeless teen.

Destruction is our end.

You have it all.

Yet you have nothing.

Did you forget?

He too was once an infant, still a child, now begging with desperate pleas.

For a moment you freeze, should I or shouldn't I?

The moment is real. You feel some unease.

You keep driving.

How quick we turn a "blind eye."

He too was once an infant, still a child, now begging with desperate pleas.

How easy we move on.

De-sense-itizing.

TOMORROW

Tomorrow brings new adventures in foreign places . . .

Tomorrow brings new lovers with charming faces.

Tomorrow brings a spirit renewed.

Tomorrow may bring a fearful future, one that is eschewed.

Tomorrow brings another breath to breathe.

Tomorrow may your heart beat beneath.

Tomorrow brings a new day.

Where I am, I will not stay.

THE CLOCK STRIKES

Tick tock goes the clock,

the little hand reaches midnight,

where has time gone, how often we hit that roadblock.

Seconds, minutes, hours later,

time never stops, time is against us.

Run from it, await Her.

Days, weeks, another season.

A sequence of events, the time in between.

The sun rises, the moon appears, babies born, people die, we live on . . .

What's your reason?

A WINTER SPELL

Cold brisk air.

Often hard to bear.

Icy roads.

A frozen river.

An unmarked path.

The sound of nothingness.

Chapped lips, dry mouth.

Runny nose.

The chafing of skin.

Emptiness.

Icicles clinging onto their rooftop until they can no longer hold on.

Bundled up, guarded.

The leaves no longer there, discarded.

Outside. Chilled.
Inside. Filled.

Still here.
Nothing to fear.

OH, LITTLE GIRL!

Time to say goodbye to that scared little girl

who'd lose herself in a dancing swirl.

An old soul lives here, residing deep within.

How far to go until you reach oblivion?

I travel alone up the mountain,

hoping to find some solace.

My legs ache as the snow melts, flowing like a fountain.

Once I reach the solemn top,

I look from up above.

Not only do I see her soaring spirit, but all that she
can envelop.

Oh, little girl, there is so much more to you,

if only you knew.

LONELINESS

I want to run from it. For most, it is hard to admit.

We must be willing to sit with it for a while.
Do not be idle or soon it may beguile.

Meandering in the past,
How I wish this feeling would not last.

The past made us who we are,
undeniably leaving you with more than a scar.

The future brings us fear.
Keeping you from those who want to draw near.

Say goodbye and let the present in.
Shed your skin.
Only then will your new life begin.

THE RECURRING DREAM

Walking through a dark winding path.

Nothing can hurt as its far too late.

Surrendering buoyantly like Sylvia Plath.

Should this be the end?

When a child lays broken, what is there left to mend?

She keeps walking until she finds the porch light.

No matter what stops her, she will put up a fight.

How unexpectedly it comes, that recurring dream.

Life worth living, now that's something to stream.

THE QUIET ONE

I am a quiet child

with a million thoughts.

I cannot sit idle.

I am a child with dreams,

I absorb all feelings,

yet I lose myself, so it seems.

Now a woman with words to say,

an imperfect body, a little awkward, a crooked smile.

A soul just as worthy

here

alive

to finally find her way.

MY EX-LOVER

Goodbye, ex-lover.

You loved me deeply I did know. Every moment you
looked at me, your love for me did show.

I'm sorry I could not give you what you needed in return.
A decade together was not time lost, but a lesson I
did learn.

They say better to have loved than to have never loved
at all.

Thank you for showing me your way of love, you were
there even when I did fall.

The time has come to no longer wallow in self-pity but to rise
above.

Goodbye, ex-lover.

Somewhat jaded and deluded.

It will find me.

I will find them.

Someone to love.

DEATH

It comes to us all.

Without prejudice.

Age,

class,

money,

beauty,

your inherited "so-called" karma.

It comes to us all.

Don't fight it.

If you live as if death is coming,

you will live to appreciate whatever age, class, money,
or beauty you have.

THE FIRE BURNS

I watch the fire burn.
Picking up my book,
the heat burns my face
with each page I turn.

I find comfort in the words of another.
Sometimes foolish, sometimes wise,
I deeply crave anything to fill the null and void,
so much I fear I will smother.

The fire burns so bright,
I lose myself in another's misadventure,
waiting for something in me to ignite.

I close another chapter,
I let the light within diminish
until there is nothing but one last ash.
My own mind is my own captor.

The fire burns bright,
to think often, to feel deeply.
Alive you are.
Never lose sight.

TIME TO LET GO

Time to let us go,
Surrender what should be and go with the flow.

Good times shared, our vulnerabilities too, oh how much we cared.

We grew together in pleasure, but somehow lost our way.
Our love we can not measure.

Letting go means goodbye to our "forever," forward we must go.
One only remains.
Simply another endeavour.

I TOLD HIM

I told him.

I told him how I felt.
He stared blankly.
Some can't speak frankly.

I am not her, nor she me.

Was I not enough?
I called his bluff.

I told him what I needed.
He did not speak.
Too scared to feel, too meek.

I told him what I wanted.
He walked away.
Most fear to speak the truth.

Lies lead us astray.

He told me goodbye.
He shut the door.
My heart

dropped

to

the

floor.

WHAT DO I WANT?

I want a million kisses that turn my days into blisses.
I want to know I am the only woman he sees . . .
In spite of my flaws, with him I settle with ease.

I want to be inspired and in return inspire,
together he and I will truly conspire.

Making the world a better place.
Whatever life gives us . . .

Together we will face.

CREATED MYTHS

Let the memories go.
Time to build new ones.
No time to revel in the woe.

No more "should haves," "what ifs?"
or telling ourselves created myths.

Easier to cry and stay as is.
Must find the strength to no longer reminisce.

One must accept chapters of life.
Lessons learned.
Time well spent.
Accept what is.
Reconcile with our internal strife.

HOLES IN MY BODY

Laying limply waiting to be cut, the mask hovers over,
closing me shut.

Hours go by. I awake to a startling shake.
There I lay, staring aimlessly ahead.
My mother waiting graciously at the tip of the bed.

Holes in my body.
Aches with each passing moment.
Not only a physical part of me gone, but a mental anguish
I've had for so long.

Am I simply shedding parts of myself to unveil the
new me?
The one waiting for so long to emerge?
Holes in my body.
From here on, I will purge.

SHADOW

It stands there.

Free as can be.
With its simple contour.
Looking back at me.

How I envy you.
Flawless.
Without doubt, cellulite, aging lines.
To trade places, I would.
In its silence, it shines.

Ominous.
Luminous.

The perfect place.
The perfect space.

The other lingers.
Held captive.
Limited.
Bound.

Somewhere in between, she may appear.

Obscure.

Why do you hide behind her?

Illuminated.
Uncertain.
Complex.
Mysterious.
It is fully you.

Not her.

The better half.

THE PALM TREE

The palm tree stands on the soft white sand
With her curved angles.

Long palms gracefully sway in the breeze.

With the blue infinite landscape as its view.

A place to take up shade, to take comfort.

With its prickly furry shells cracked open,

revealing the milky white, pouring over,

giving life only to those who dare to climb to its peak.

With its unwitting beauty, soft, yet standing firmly in
its depth.

Tides beating against it, whatever chaos surrounds—

The unexpected tempest, the blazing sun, the thrashing
of waves.

Sea salt resting on her leaves, cleansing whatever seaweed
has washed up below.

Above she stands.

In all her glory.

Narrow yet curvy.

Imperfect.

Yet perfectly adorned.

Tender.

Easily swayed.

Complete.

Utterly sure

she can,

she will,

withstand

any storm.

MY ONE TRUE LOVE

My lovers, each one so different than the other.
Each one revealing a part of myself to me,
peeling my layers, slowly becoming free.

The first . . . kind and gentle.
Souls made for one another,
soft and sentimental.

My second, strong and sensitive altogether.
In his fragility lies his greatest strength.
In me he saw such a treasure.
I wonder if I kept him at arm's length?

The third like the sea and moon attune.
Not afraid to share the depth of his soul.
Yet, he had to leave so soon.

And so, I still wander about . . . where is my other half
to help make me whole?

Am I not complete just as I am?
Is the love I've had just a sham?

My one true love . . .

Do I ask for too much? Or not enough?

Maybe it's time to call my bluff?

My one true love . . .

NOT WITH ME

I noticed you're everywhere but with me.

Seeing and sailing the world, the one I am no longer a part of.

Did you tell her too, all the places we'd go and all that we could be?

Some wisdom to you I wish to impart:

I made you stronger and better for her.

You made me stronger and better for him.

It was I, not you, the unrelenting anchor.

THE OLIVE TREE

Basil and oregano,
brewing homemade tomato sauce in my mother's kitchen.
New Dalton Rose chinaware
sitting in a wooden cabinet, finely crafted by my
father's hands.
Our strong limbs of the olive tree deeply rooted into
the earth.

With one piece of luggage in hand,
only pocket change in his newly purchased cotton pants.
Dignified.
With his fine Italian leather shoes,
a symbol of his pride.

Embarking on an over-crowded ship to a vast,
uncharted land.

Cold, desolate, and alone.

Back home, a new bride awaits.
Walking the cobblestone streets, greeting familiar faces,
running home to be welcomed by love letters.

Like those in the movies, written in perfect calligraphy,
endless P.S.'s
an epic love story, or at least that's what we make of it.
Letters from a million miles, snow-capped mountains,
lakes and oceans, making their way through the breeze.
A tiny warm village with the Mediterranean Sea gently
sitting at its horizon.

Like a nestling with its beak peeking upward eagerly awaiting its mother. Its next meal.
The innocent bride waits, patiently, uncertain,
naïve, trusting.

Years passing by.

His calloused, tired hands, proof of his committed love,
not only to his craft but to his future life with his devoted
bride to be.

Her meticulous hand-embroidered shawls wrapping her
with hope from the winter humid air hovering nearby.

Cold, desolate, and alone.

Until one day, they meet again.
Only stronger than before.
Bitter, sweet espresso sizzling on the stovetop.
The olive tree stands strong.
Enduring.
No longer
cold, desolate, and alone.

WITHOUT CONDITIONS

If I told you I wanted you to let me love you, would you?
I can give you my trust.
I can give you my word.
Your voice will not go unheard.
I can give you my care.
I can give you my body.
Your life and mine to share.
I can give you my passion for life.
I can give you my respect.
I can give you my time.
I can give you my loyalty
without reason or rhyme.
Without conditions.

In all your glory.
In all your story.

In all my glory.
In all my story.

Without conditions.

MY ITALIAN LOVE AFFAIR

Oh, how much I adore you.

From top to bottom.
My eyes follow you.

From here to there, a rolling landscape.
Green pastures.
The scent of oranges and lemons.
Steep valorous valleys hiding idyllic villages.
Green to black olives hanging from their lance-like leaves.

Rocky cliffs to sandy shores.
Deep dark caves
with crevices to explore.
Sparkling coastal coves calmly caressing turquoise waters.
Mountain ranges embraced by each passing season.
So much to uncover.

With hundreds of fruits that filled bellies.
Feet that have fought and stepped on this earth a thou-
sand times.
The whistling sea winds witness to a million lovers.

The beating southern sun.
Warmth on my skin.
A labyrinth of winding streets.
Archways leading me to the unsteady doorstep of your
weathered door.

I had to leave.

On my own.

A dead end.
No other choice.

The mind thinks it knows best.
The heart feels what is best.

And I came back to you.

My Italian love affair.

I FEEL YOU

I feel you.
Adoring the crimson sky resting its glorious sun on the
horizon to meet the end of day.
Standing in silence as snowflakes somberly drift to
the ground.
Hearing the giggles of a baby gazing past me as if
embraced by a bright light.
Driving in a treacherous storm, sitting next to me as I hold
the grip of my steering wheel.
Rising with the morning sun as the dew drops from its
blades of grass.
Walking on an autumn day as I smell the cindery sweetness
of each leaf floating from the crisp air.
Reflecting in the peaceful stillness of a lake.
Summoning the soothing rhythm of waves who
welcome the sea to its shore.
Echoing whispers as I climb to the mountain peaks
from valleys and meadows.
Gazing at the luminous star-filled night, with the moon
smirking back at me.

You are near.

A door left slightly open,
a telephone ring with no answer,
a flickering light,
an unexpected butterfly fluttering its wings,
I feel you.

I can't see you. I can't touch you.
Your body just a shell holding you in.
You were and are so much more.
The emptiness itself is death.
But I know you are there.

I feel you.
And to feel is more than to see.

More powerful
More beautiful
More real
than ever before!

A NOTE TO MY LINGERING TEENAGE SELF:

If someone is going to deeply and truly love you,
It will never have anything to do with how you look.

My flat chest,
with my scrawny arms guarding me in.
My wider than wide gum receding smile,
with silvery shimmering braces.
My bulging eyes
with their naiveté looking out into the world.
My skinny chicken legs that can run faster than yours.
My spotty oily skin
with pimples waiting to be free.
The way I try to hide behind it all.

You will love me for the depth and breadth of my soul.
You will love me for every inch of my idiosyncratic ways.
You will love me just as imperfect as I am,
because you will know there is more to me than what
you see.

And if you can't see what I see, then who is the imperfect
one after all?

ONE SWEET POMEGRANATE

One sweet pomegranate

emerges from its branch.

A tiny seed, into many more seeds it becomes.

Relentless, through time it overcomes.

Each seed more fulfilling than the other.

Miraculous rare fruit you are.

A glorious abundant shrub.

More like a trub!

A masterpiece indeed.

The right time, the right season.

Found in the rarest of places.

Look deep between spaces.

Warm.

Temperate.

In its wild orchard it waits.

Many fates await.

Tough to break into.

Delicate at its core.

More than just an apple, orange, or even a lemon.

Serene without venom.

Succulent.

Juicy.

It's soft, brain-like interior, complex, tender.

A fruit to remember.

More than a mouthful of 613 seeds.

Zesty with just the right zang.

Sometimes yellow.

Hanging mellow.

Sometimes green.

At its full bloom

a damasked red.

No longer dormant or dead.

Once she falls into your hands,

take gentle care,

if you dare.

Completely yours to enjoy.

Bound to bring you joy.

One sweet pomegranate.

9 781525 571534